SPINOZA IN 90 MINUTES

Spinoza
IN 90 MINUTES

Paul Strathern

IVAN R. DEE

Library of Congress Cataloging-in-Publication Data:
Strathern, Paul, 1940–
    Spinoza in 90 minutes / Paul Strathern
      p. cm. — (Philosophers in 90 minutes)
    Includes bibliographical references and index.
    ISBN 1-56663-215-3 (pbk. : alk. paper). —
ISBN 1-56663-214-5 (cloth : alk. paper)
    1. Spinoza, Benedictus de, 1632–1677. I. Title. II. Series.
B3998.S83   1998
199'.492—dc21   98-36086

Contents

SPINOZA IN 90 MINUTES

Introduction

Spinoza is the philosopher's philosopher. He constructed a metaphysical system of astonishing brilliance and beauty, which is all the more astonishing for being derived neither from reality nor experience. He was a deeply religious man, though apparently practicing no particular faith. His philosophy is permeated with the idea of God, and he lived the life of a saint. Consequently he was abominated by all religions during his lifetime, and after his death his works were vilified, vigorously prosecuted, and burned.

Nowadays, when philosophers are not required to believe in God, live scandalous lives like the rest of us, and are expected to pay some attention to reality, Spinoza is held up as a philosophic exemplar. Perhaps if he is eventually canonized, he will become the patron saint of hypocrites.

The core of Spinoza's philosophy is his all-embracing system. This straddles the hierarchical world of medieval certainty and the emerging belief in the power of reason alone to reach the truth. His mathematically generated system embodied *Deus sive Natura* (God or Nature). It started from basic assumptions, and by a series of geometric proofs constructed a universe which was also God. His is the classic example of pantheism: the belief that God and the universe are one and the same thing. This has a curious echo in the modern Gaia hypothesis, where our planet is viewed as a single vast organism or self-regulating cell. Spinoza's system also yielded a holistic ethics similar to that favored by modern ecologists. Harm the world and you harm God; harm another and you harm yourself.

Spinoza's political theory was equally ahead of its time. He believed that the purpose of the state was only to protect the individual, in order that he could freely develop himself and his ideas by use of enlightened reason.

Spinoza's systematic theistic approach renders his philosophy an anachronistic oddity. Ironically, the conclusions he drew from this out-of-date system are deeply in accord with modern thought—from science to politics. Both his system, and the conclusions he drew from it, have a compelling beauty unequaled in the history of philosophy. If beauty were truth, and truth beauty, as Keats claimed, Spinoza's philosophy would be all we know and all we need to know.

Spinoza's Life and Works

Baruch (or Benedict) de Spinoza was born on November 4, 1632, in Amsterdam. He was descended from Portuguese Sephardic Jews—his name derives from the town of Espinoza in northwestern Spain. His family had emigrated to Holland, where they were able to shed the crypto-Christianity forced on them under the Inquisition and return to the Judaism of their forebears. Spinoza's father was a successful merchant who lived in a smart house on Burgwal near the Old Portuguese Synagogue. His mother, who was also from Portugal, died in childbirth when he was six. Spinoza's childhood appears to have been blighted by family bereavements.

When he was twenty-two his father died, having buried three wives and four of his children.

Spinoza was educated in the stifling Jewish fashion of the period, spending hours each day in the study of the Bible (the Christian Old Testament) and the Talmud, the authoritative body of Jewish tradition. Despite the excruciating boredom of this severely limited curriculum, Spinoza appears to have enjoyed his studies, and his father assumed that he would become a rabbi. Outside school hours the young Spinoza was encouraged to take lessons in Latin and ancient Greek. Reality and the modern world appear to have played as little a part in his education as they were to play in his philosophy. But Baruch Spinoza was no young fogey. Jewish students of an independent turn of mind were beginning to chafe against the strictures of orthodoxy. They felt that their spiritual requirements had developed beyond those of a tribe of prehistoric Asiatic nomads, and they began questioning the Bible.

The leaders of the Jewish community were becoming deeply worried by this tendency. The

United Provinces of the Netherlands was a tolerant society—but only compared with the Ku Klux Klan mentality prevailing elsewhere in Europe. (It was the Spanish Inquisition of this period that provided the Ku Klux Klan with its dunces' uniform.) Jews were still not citizens in Holland, and attacks by Jews on the Bible were liable to be seen as attacks on Christianity.

So the reaction of Jewish authorities was hardly sympathetic when Spinoza began hanging around outside the synagogue peddling his unorthodox views. According to him, the authors of the Pentateuch (the opening five books of the Bible) were scientific simpletons, and weren't much better as theologians. As if this wasn't enough, the twenty-two-year-old Spinoza also began arguing that there was no evidence in the Bible to prove that God had a body, that the soul was immortal, or that angels existed (presumably Jacob's wrestling match had been a sort of epileptic fit).

Spinoza was an extremely bright young man, and it was virtually impossible to argue with him—so the authorities decided to try a different tack. At first they attempted to silence him with vague threats; but when they saw that Spinoza was far too headstrong for this to work, they offered him an annuity of 1,000 florins to go away and keep his ideas to himself. (In those days a student could live for a year on 2,000 florins.) Considering the seriousness of Spinoza's blasphemies, this was an amazingly lenient approach by the Jewish authorities. But Spinoza spurned their generous offer. This is usually held up as an example of his saintly refusal to be deterred from telling the truth. The seventeenth-century Jewish community of Amsterdam may be forgiven for viewing it otherwise. What could they do to shut him up?

One evening as Spinoza was leaving the Portuguese Synagogue, a man stepped up beside him. In the nick of time Spinoza noticed the raised dagger in his hand and backed, holding up his cloaked arm to protect himself. The dagger slashed through Spinoza's cloak, but he himself was unhurt (and is said to have kept the slashed cloak "as a memorial"). The man responsible for this attack is usually represented as a fanatic, and it's quite possible that he was. On the other hand, he too might have been a man of selfless courage—taking it upon himself to rid the community of a dangerous threat by committing a crime for which he would almost certainty be caught and hung. Saintliness and martyrdom can both require a similar arrogance.

As if this wasn't enough, Spinoza now sent a long open letter to the synagogue authorities. In this he outlined in precise detail his views, backing them up with a series of logical arguments which he claimed were irrefutable.

The synagogue authorities decided that they now had no alternative: they would have to demonstrate to the Christian community that they no longer had anything to do with this Spinoza. As far as they were concerned, Spinoza was now a nonperson, an ex-Jew. In July 1656 a grand ceremony of excommunication was held, and Spinoza was banished in style from the Jewish community. The great horn was blown, the candles were extinguished one by one, and the curse was read out: "With the judgment of the angels and the saints we hereby excommunicate, execrate, and anathematize Baruch de Espinoza. Cursed be he by day and cursed be he by night, cursed in his lying down and cursed in his rising up, cursed in going out and cursed in coming in. The Lord shall destroy his name under the sun and cut him off for his undoing from all the tribes of Israel. None may speak with him by word of mouth nor by writing nor shew any favor to him, nor be under one roof with him, nor come within four cubits of him, nor read any document written or dictated by him." With such a recommendation, it is little surprise that Spinoza's writings remain eagerly sought after by Jewish (and Gentile) readers to this day.

Meanwhile this left the twenty-three-year-old Spinoza in a bit of a fix. His father had died a year earlier, leaving him all the cash. Whereupon, in the time-honored fashion (popular with Jew and Gentile alike), the family had bitterly disputed the will. Spinoza's half-sister Rebekah had sued, claiming that the entire estate was by rights hers.

Being a saint, Spinoza had no need of all this unearned lucre. But he was also a philosopher;

16

and as such he found it quite unthinkable that he should be defeated in an argument. So Spinoza contested the case. After wasting everyone's time and earning the lawyers the usual fat fee, Spinoza won the case—and then informed his sister that she could have the lot anyway (except for a four-poster bed, with curtains for privacy, which he rather fancied for himself). Having run through the entire gamut of philosophical gestures, Spinoza now found himself as good as broke. And after the excommunication ceremony he no longer even had a good Jewish home for his bed.

Spinoza was forced to put up with a Christian friend called Affinius van den Ende, who ran a private school in his home. Van den Ende was a former Jesuit priest turned liberal. He was a man of wide learning, especially in the classics, and besides being a schoolmaster also rather fancied himself as a poet and playwright. Affinius van den Ende College (Close to the End College) had a good name in the community, though a number of overanxious parents had recently removed their children when they suspected they were being taught to think for themselves. Free-thinking was officially considered absolutely intolerable; but unofficially it was looked upon as just part of the educational process, a phase which the pupils soon grew out of, much as they do now.

Spinoza earned his keep by teaching in van den Ende's small private school. He also took the opportunity of attending a number of the classes: improving his Latin and Greek, quickly catching up on mathematics, and acquainting himself with the Scholastic view of Aristotelian philosophy. Around this time he began studying the commentaries on Aristotle by the great Jewish scholars Moses ben Maimon (usually known to us as Maimonides) and Chasdai Creskas of Saragossa (usually not known to us at all). The latter held the view that matter was eternal and that the Creation was simply the imposition of order upon it—a doctrine which was heavily to influence Spinoza's own philosophy.

In the evenings van den Ende introduced Spinoza to the latest writings of Descartes, which were now revolutionizing philosophy.

Descartes's rigidly mechanistic view of the workings of the universe was to play a decisive role in Spinoza's thinking, though he was to ignore the modern subjective component of Descartes's philosophy (which had made it so revolutionary in the first place). It was probably at this time that Spinoza also read the great sixteenth-century free spirit and original thinker Giordano Bruno, whose curious blend of occult ideas and advanced scientific thought enabled him to achieve the distinction of being excommunicated by both the Protestants and the Catholics (who also burned him at the stake for good measure). Once again Spinoza ignored the dazzlingly original aspects of this philosophy (as well as some fantastic Black Magic) in favor of Bruno's metaphysical belief in an infinite and pantheistic universe. One by one Spinoza was assembling the ingredients which when cooked in the hot oven of his intellect were to produce the unsurpassed confectionery of his philosophy: a creation of infinite sweetness, containing a mouth-watering variety of philosophical cherries, plum observations, and sickly theological

19

cream, all overlaid with marzipantheism and coated with rigid geometric icing, topped by the single glowing candle of its uniqueness. (We will discover later what all this tasted like.)

But at this stage Spinoza was sweet on more than philosophy. He is said to have fallen in love with van den Ende's daughter Clara Maria. Judging from the portraits and descriptions we have of Spinoza, he may well have created a slightly odd impression in later life. But in the young man these genius mannerisms were almost certainly still dormant. Sources speak of him being short, with a swarthy complexion and black curly hair. "One might easily know by his looks that he was descended from Portuguese Jews," says one, while another speaks of him having the appearance of a "Sephardic Grandee."

Clara Maria van den Ende taught classics and music at her father's school. According to one source, "She was none of the most beautiful, but she had a great deal of Wit, a jovial Humor and a great Capacity" (for what, is not specified). Unfortunately she fell for one of her students, a young man called Dirck Kerckrinck, whom she ended up marrying.

Other sources dismiss this story, pointing out that Clara Maria was only twelve at the time. Whether or not Humbert Spinoza fell for Clara Lolita, other evidence suggests that Spinoza was not the sexually dormant genius figure so beloved of his early hagiographers. Unique among the great philosophers, Spinoza was to write with penetrating psychological awareness about love and sexual jealousy. In his *Ethics* he proposes: "The stronger the emotion which we imagine the person we love to feel for us, the more we are filled with self-pride." In the ensuing proposition he insists: "If anyone thinks that there is between his beloved and another person the same or a more intimate feeling of love than there was between them when he alone loved her, he will feel hatred for the one he loved and be gripped with envy for his rival." And he goes on to define jealousy as "the swings of feeling arising from the simultaneous experience of love and hatred, together with bitter envy for a third person."

The man who wrote these words had certainly suffered the emotions they describe. And it seems unlikely they were all on account of a twelve-year-old girl. Why? In his *Treatise on the Correction of Understanding,* Spinoza mentions, without giving specific details, a traumatic experience which transformed his life: "I understood myself plunged into great peril and in dire need of pursuing a remedy, however uncertain its outcome, with all my energy. I was like a sick man with a fatal disease, who is faced with death if he does not find a cure." This prompted him to divert his energies toward "love for the eternal and infinite which alone feeds the mind pleasure and frees it from all pain. For this reason it is much to be desired and should be sought with all our might." (This love occurs in Spinoza's philosophy as one of his most uplifting poetic concepts: *amor intellectualis dei*—the intellectual love of God.) From what we know of Spinoza, it seems unlikely that he would have viewed heterosexual love as a "fatal disease" which had to be avoided with "all our might." But any further Freudian conjectures would need to be based on more knowledge than we actually have of his life and personality.

Not long after the putative episode with Clara, the van den Ende College closed down—when its headmaster unexpectedly disappeared to France, in the time-honored manner of private school headmasters. Here he eventually came to a sorry end when he involved himself in an inept plot to overthrow Louis XIV and set up a utopian republic, which resulted in him being publicly hanged.

Sometime during the 1650s Spinoza began to learn the trade of lens-grinding. Lenses were much in demand in Holland at the time. They were needed for microscopes in the expanding diamond trade, nautical telescopes, and reading spectacles (which, like 1000cc motorcycles today, were rapidly becoming a fashionable accoutrement of middle age). After giving up teaching, Spinoza was to support himself financially by grinding lenses for the rest of his life. It is said that he became highly adept at this trade, and that his lenses were much sought after. The former claim may well be just a piece of mythology, but we know for certain that the latter is true, though in a way which didn't benefit Spinoza in the least. During the nineteenth century, when the selling of mementos of the famous became something of a boom industry, an Amsterdam antique dealer named Cornelius van Halewijn began selling lenses ground by Spinoza to wealthy Jewish businessmen, visiting German professors, and other collectors. These period lenses were not of a particularly high quality, and it's now been calculated that van Halewijn must have sold several hundred of them. Perhaps he stumbled across a warehouse full of lenses which Spinoza hadn't quite finished working on.

Spinoza now retired to the country to do some serious grinding. Lenses and original ideas began to appear in equal number. By this time his few friends were largely Remonstrants, a Christian sect similar to the Mennonites, whose independent, God-fearing ways succeeded in uniting all other Dutch Christians against them. It was also around this time that Spinoza Christianized his name to Benedict (which, like

Baruch, also means blessed). But there's no suggestion that he became a Christian.

Spinoza eventually found lodgings with a Remonstrant surgeon named Hermann Homan in the village of Rijnsburg, which in those days was a remote spot on the banks of the Rhine outside Leyden. This house still stands, opposite a potato patch, in the quiet suburban street now known as Spinozalaan. Spinoza's room must have looked out over the flat countryside of fields and canals which still stretch beneath the grey skies toward the distant horizon. Here Spinoza wrote two works which were to be seminal to his entire philosophy. One was a "geometric version" of Descartes's *Principles of Philosophy*. This was the vast, rambling work that the French philosopher had produced toward the end of his life, into which he had poured all his philosophic and scientific theories. Spinoza's idea was to transform Descartes's thinking into a series a geometric proofs, which everyone would immediately be able to see were either right or wrong. Spinoza was deeply affected by Descartes's thinking, which had transformed philosophy in a more drastic way than any other philosopher has achieved before or since. But if Spinoza was to do good and original philosophy of his own, it was imperative for him to distance himself from the over-whelming influence of Descartes. This he achieved by reducing Descartes's delightful and lucid style to a rubble of almost impenetrable mathematics.

The other book Spinoza wrote at this time was *A Short Treatise on God, Man and His Well-Being.* Written in Dutch, it contains many of the ideas which were soon to appear in his mature philosophy. Unfortunately, when Spinoza came to write this philosophy he decided against writing it in easily readable Dutch, and instead chose Latin, contorting this into the "geometric" style to which he had reduced Descartes's work. This has rendered his masterpiece, the *Ethics,* virtually unreadable. The entire work is broken up like a piece of Euclidian geometry into a se-ries of definitions, axioms, propositions, and proofs. Viz:

Definition
1. A book is defined as something you can read.
2. Style is defined as the way in which an author chooses to write a book.
Axioms
1. We read a book because we are interested in finding out what the author has to say.
2. The style of a book plays a major role in its readability.
Proposition
This style is unreadable.
Proof
It is likely that most people have already given up reading this proof. (See Axiom 1.) If you have read this far, it is certain that you will not read much farther if I continue to use this style. (See Axiom 2.) Therefore this style is unreadable. Q.E.D.

And so on, for more than two hundred pages. Even *Shipwrecked Prisoner of Six Virgins* couldn't withstand this kind of treatment. Not surprisingly, few managed to reach the end of the *Ethics* (Part V. Proposition XLII, with its proof, which involves references to five previous propositions, one previous definition, and the corollaries to two further proofs. Q.E.D.). One person who did manage to make it to the end, Leibniz, claimed that although Spinoza's entire philosophic system is closely linked, not all its proofs follow one another with precise mathematical rigor. So there are a few unexpected twists in the plot; you just have to know where to look for them.

But what precisely is the plot? Spinoza starts with eight definitions. These set out the basic assumptions of his universe and his philosophy. They define:

1. a thing which is its own cause
2. a thing which is finite in its own kind
3. substance
4. its attributes
5. its modes
6. God
7. Freedom
8. Eternity

As we can see from the very nature of these definitions, Spinoza starts by regarding the world from an extremely rational and abstract point of view. This becomes even more apparent when we look at some of the definitions themselves:

—"A thing which is its own cause (*causa sui*) I understand as something whose essence involves existence and whose nature cannot be conceived except as existing."

—"A thing is finite (*in suo genere finito*) when it can be limited by another thing of the same nature. For example, a body is said to be finite because we can always conceive of another, larger body. Similarly, a thought is limited by another thought. However, body cannot be limited by thought, nor thought by body."

Spinoza goes on to define two concepts which are all-important for his system: God and Eternity.

—"By God (*Deus*) I understand an absolutely infinite Being—that is, a substance consisting of infinite attributes, each of which expresses eternal and infinite essence.

—"By Eternity (*aeternitas*) I understand existence itself, conceived as following necessarily from the definition of the thing which is eternal.

"*Explanation:* For existence so conceived is an eternal truth, inasmuch as it is the essence of the eternal thing: therefore it cannot be explained by duration or time, although duration can be conceived as without beginning or end."

From these definitions Spinoza proceeds by way of Euclidian proofs to construct a necessary, deterministic, and irrefutable system which includes the entire universe. Every feature of existence is logically necessary, and every consistent logical possibility must exist. (Modern physics has now shown that logically inconsistent systems can also exist—as in the quantum theory of light—so Spinoza's universe would today be in the dark.)

Spinoza's universe was pantheistic—that is, the universe is God, and vice versa. He refers to it as *Deus sive Natura:* God or Nature. This is the only substance. But this God-Universe has an infinite number of attributes. We are capable of perceiving only two of these attributes: extension and thought. These two attributes make up our world, much like two dimensions, and we remain unaware of the infinite (minus two) remaining dimensions.

Spinoza manages to overcome the great problem which defeated Descartes, namely, how does the mind (which works by reason) interact with the body (which works by mechanics)? According to Spinoza's system: "Mind and body are the same individual which is conceived now under the attribute of thought, and now under the attribute of extension." Mind and Body are merely different aspects of the same thing—*Deus sive Natura* perceived under just two of His infinite attributes.

Our apprehension is limited to just two of God's infinite attributes, but these both conform to the logic of the whole. "The order and connection of ideas is the same as the order and connection of things." Cause and effect are linked as rigidly and irreversibly as the processes of reason. Thus, in the vastness of Spinoza's infinite universe, cause and effect become part of a greater *logical* necessity. Our world of extension is logically determined, its chains of cause and effect are logically necessary, irreversible, and undivertable (no different from the necessary sequence of logic which takes place in the mind). In just the same way, finite things proceed necessarily from infinite substance. Yet they remain part of *Deus sive Natura* (God or Nature).

Under such circumstances it may appear superfluous to ask: How do we know this divine being exists? Consider the world we perceive if such a divine being did not exist. Without this backup we would inhabit a world devoid of metaphysical substance, a blindly unfolding universe. Nowadays many of us feel able to live with such a world, but Spinoza could not. He needed to prove the existence of his *Deus sive Natura*. And to do this he chose a proof characteristic of his ambivalent stance between the hierarchy of medieval certainty and the brave new world of the emerging Age of Reason.

The Ontological Argument was a medieval favorite for proving the existence of God. Put simply, it stated that the idea of God is the greatest possible idea of which we can conceive. If this idea doesn't include the attribute of existence, then there must be an even greater idea exactly like it which does. Thus the greatest of all possible ideas must exist, otherwise an even greater idea would be possible. Q.E.D. God exists. Spinoza used several variations of this argument in his discussion of the unique infinite substance which he identified as "God or Nature." First he takes the thought of substance: "So if someone says that he has a clear and distinct—that is to say, true—idea of substance and that he nevertheless doubts if such a substance exists, this would be just the same as if he said that he has a true idea but nevertheless suspects it may be false." From this it follows: "Since existence appertains to the nature of substance, its definition must of necessity involve existence, and therefore from its mere definition its existence can be concluded."

So much medieval sophistry? Skeptics of this approach should note that it remains very much a part of modern thinking. Contemporary scientists have proposed a similar argument to account for several central notions, including the existence of the Big Bang and the elusive

Theory of Everything (or unified theory). No less a figure than Stephen Hawking asked: "Is the unified theory so compelling that it brings about its own existence?" Such argument suggests the inevitable conclusion: the universe must be the way it is, and had to be created, because no other universe (or lack of one) was possible. Spinoza would certainly have recognized this metaphysical argument. And as a supreme metaphysical idea, Spinoza's *Deus sive Natura* belongs in the Big Bang category. Its Euclidian mathematics may have been superseded, but its compelling beauty remains undeniable.

Despite Spinoza's determined geometric efforts, his metaphysical system exhibits many profoundly poetic features. Suffice to mention but a few: The aim of the wise should be to try and see the universe as God sees it *sub specie aeternitatis* ("beneath the aspect of eternity"). Every human body is part of God's body, thus when we harm others we harm ourselves. The happiness of each of us depends on the happiness of all. The universe cannot be explained by

34

reference to anything else—even God, because it is God. The universe is thus without meaning, yet at the same time is its own meaning.

Many of Spinoza's ideas have a deep resonance and are illuminating to those who neither believe in God nor his system. His theory of emotions is particularly prescient. Unlike so many pre-twentieth-century philosophical theories, Spinoza's does not appear inadequate or naive (or just plain wrong) in the light of modern psychology. Desire is defined as "the very essence of man." And "pleasure is man's transition from a state of less perfection to a state of greater perfection." Pain is the opposite. Spinoza goes on to state: "Wonder is the thought of any thing on which the mind stays fixed because this particular thought has no connection with any others." Consider this in the light of Plato's celebrated dictum: "Philosophy begins in wonder." It is not difficult to imagine Spinoza, wrapt in wonder, contemplating his God, who has no connection with any other thing because he is *everything*. But his definition of love as "pleasure accompanied by the idea of an external

35

cause" would not seem to accord with his conception of *amor intellectualis dei* (the intellectual love of God). In Spinoza's view (and the view of modern psychology), this intellectual love of God would necessarily include an element of self-love—if God and all Nature are the same thing. And this element would not have an external cause. Spinoza attempts to defend himself against this charge by maintaining: "The mind's intellectual love of God is part of the infinite love by which God loves himself." But this would only seem to confirm the flaw in his argument.

Despite such apparent inconsistencies, his theory goes on to "prove" several profound insights. "There is no hope without fear and no fear without hope." Both confidence and despair arise "from the idea of a thing future or past concerning which reason for doubt has been removed."

However, this same matter of doubt (and error) reveals a serious flaw in Spinoza's philosophy. Spinoza himself had no doubts about the truth and certainty of his thought: "I do not presume that I have found the best philosophy, but I know that I think the true one. If you ask me how I know this, I shall answer, in the same way that you know that the three angles of a triangle are equal to two right angles." Spinoza viewed doubt and error in a Neoplatonic manner, considering them to be a natural absence or lack in our apprehension of the truth. In other words, doubt and error were in fact unreal, being inadequate or incomplete apprehensions of the truth (which was the only reality). This account is no more adequate than his claim to geometric certainty for his philosophy. (And although he could not have known it, in the non-Euclidian geometry of curved surfaces, the three angles of a triangle are not invariably equal to two right angles.)

According to Spinoza: "the endeavor after self-preservation is the primary and only foundation of virtue." Unfortunately, if self-preservation is primary, how is it possible to account for suicide? Spinoza said that in this case "external and hidden causes . . . may so affect the body as to cause it to put on another nature contrary to that which it had at first." In other words, suicide is inhuman, and a person is behaving as something other than a human being when he commits suicide. This, like the theory of doubt, is scarcely adequate. But these are minor flaws in a system of great wisdom and insight. Indeed, the subtlety of Spinoza's understanding (and lack of blunders) becomes even more astonishing in light of his insistence on geometry *in all circumstances:* "I regard human actions and desires exactly as if I were dealing with lines, plane surfaces, or solids."

In keeping with this approach, Spinoza himself appears to have adopted a somewhat detached attitude toward the world which we lesser human beings inhabit. According to a contemporary, "He seemed to live completely within himself, always solitary, as if lost in his thoughts." Indeed, sometimes "he would not leave his house for three months at a time." (Anyone who has experienced a frigid grey Dutch winter, or looked closely at those seventeenth-century Dutch paintings of icebound canals, may not find this so eccentric.) Outside his all-absorbing work his pleasures were few but revealing. In the words of an early biographer: "He would collect spiders and set them to fight with one another," or using a magnifying glass he would "find some flies, place them in a spider's web, and study the ensuing struggle with great pleasure, even laughing out loud on occasion." In a letter to a friend, Spinoza declared, "Everyone observes with admiration and delight in animals the very things which he detests and regards with aversion in men." His wisdom concerning human nature appears to have been confined to his philosophy.

Yet philosophy, despite the etymological roots of its name, is not interested in the love of wisdom. Philosophy is a serious business, and as with any other such, you only stay in business by slaughtering the opposition. The moment Spinoza's system appeared, every philosopher worth his salt went straight for the jugular. Unfortunately Spinoza's entire system stands or falls on those initial definitions, upon which the whole edifice is constructed. If you disprove Spinoza's definition of substance, that's it. No substance, no universe. So how does Spinoza define substance?

"*Definition*. I understand by SUBSTANCE (*substantia*) that which is in itself and is conceived by itself; that is, whose concept needs the concept of no other thing for it to be formed from."

To expect philosophers to agree on even something as basic (though craftily worded) as this, was naive of Spinoza. But worse was to come once the theologians started reading the *Ethics*. If God is merely the deterministic universe, this denies God's transcendence. It also does away with his personality (along with that famous wrath), as well as his free will to choose whether to obey his own laws (the laws of nature, science, etc.) or change his mind (miracles, acts of God, etc.). According to Spinoza's conception, we can love God as much as we like, but there's no way he can love us in return. This left a lot of people feeling deeply unloved and facing the prospect of all their holiness going unrewarded. By rendering all things holy, Spinoza was to unleash an unholy row.

Fortunately Spinoza realized this might happen, and his *Ethics* was published posthumously. During his lifetime it was distributed only clandestinely among his philosophic friends. One of these, who also lived at Rijnsburg, did not behave so prudently—which served as a warning to Spinoza. When Adrian Koerbach published his book *Light in Dark Places,* which attacked contemporary religion, medical practice, and the prevailing moral climate, he was hauled before the courts. Here the prosecutor called for the seizure of all his possessions, his right thumb to be cut off, his tongue to be pierced with a red-hot poker, and a prison sentence of thirty years. Koerbach must have felt quite relieved when he was only fined 6,000 florins and given ten years' hard labor followed by exile. This shows the sort of trouble you could get into by publicly preaching the wrong ideas, even in liberal Holland (whose moral tolerance was without equal in Europe and indeed throughout the world except in the South Seas and the pirate kingdoms of the West Indies). Adrian Koerbach was specifically asked at his trial whether he had in any way been influenced by the ideas of Spinoza—a charge he denied (though whether this was due to professional pride or commendable decency is unclear). Spinoza could see which way the wind was blowing.

In 1663 Spinoza moved to Voorburg, an outer suburb of The Hague, and was to live in this city for the rest of his life. In a letter he wrote a couple of years later, he makes his only known intentional reference to himself. (Other references, such as those regarding insectlike human behavior and the woes of jealousy, were not intended as self-revealing remarks. These were Philosophy, or The Philosopher speaking—from within his detached winter quarters.) Writing to a physician friend, Spinoza tells how he has unsuccessfully tried to remedy a fever by bleeding himself (presumably with leeches, the common medical practice of the period). He goes on to say that he is looking forward to receiving a pot of his friend's red rose jam, and that he has also got over an attack of the ague: "by dint of good diet I at last drove it out and sent it packing, where it has gone I know not, but I am taking care that it shall not come back." Despite this feeble joke (the unique example of this species in all Spinoza's writing), it looks as if Spinoza was rather worried about his health. He appears to have had a rather frail constitution, which was beset by a string of minor ailments—such as would have been the envy of a hypochondriac like Descartes (who had departed fifteen years previously for the great medicine chest in the sky).

Spinoza lived a very simple life, boarding in a single room. Here he not only slept and wrote but apparently quite often did his lens-grinding too. It doesn't take much imagination to picture the sheaves of paper and opened books covered in a thin layer of glass dust. And it's possible that here too he had a small latticed window with a view out over the flat fields of potato patches and canals beneath the gloomy grey skies. (This might also have provided a useful source of flies for his resident spiders.)

According to one source, Spinoza often "lived all day on a milk sop done with butter, and a pot of beer." And on another day he might subsist on "gruel done with raisins and butter."

According to the same source, he drank only two half-pints of wine in a month—which would have constituted heroic abstinence in the Holland of his day. Although one suspects that he took even this only to fortify his blood. Spinoza is said to have described his way of life as "just making both ends meet, like a snake with its tail in its mouth."

Now in his early thirties, Spinoza had lost the arrogance of his youth. This is usually put down to the spiritually beneficial effects of blossoming genius, though in most cases when genius bursts into full exotic bloom the effect is precisely the opposite (megalomania and solipsism being the usual occupational hazards of this tantrum-bedeviled state). In fact, Spinoza's loss of arrogance was probably due to the slow but inexorable realization that his great philosophy, to which he had devoted his entire life, could never achieve widespread recognition during his lifetime. All hope of publication gradually faded. A grinding humiliation capable of extinguishing all manner of pride.

Even so, Spinoza felt the need to explain himself: to demonstrate to the world, and especially to his religious opponents, that his philosophy was not incompatible with orthodox belief in God. So when he had finished writing the *Ethics,* he started into a new work called *Tractatus Theologico-Politicus,* a treatise on theology and politics. Spinoza's *Tractatus* is an odd work, a blend of political theory and biblical commentary. He told his friends he was trying to prepare the way for the eventual publication of the *Ethics* by demonstrating that "the liberty to philosophize is compatible with devout piety and with the peace of the state." Spinoza was perhaps the greatest of all philosophical rationalists, but at this point it's difficult to be persuaded that he was arguing rationally. His impersonal pantheistic God bears no relation to the Jehovah of the Bible, and his theory that when we harm others we harm ourselves squared with neither contemporary religious attitudes (toward heretics and unbelievers) nor contemporary political and moral attitudes (toward almost anyone). And his view that the miracles of the Bible were simply natural events, which had been deliberately misinterpreted for purposes of religious propaganda, was unlikely to win his book many glowing reviews in the church press.

Be this as it may, Spinoza has some interesting (and surprisingly modern) things to say about political theory. His thinking was in many ways a response to the English philosopher Thomas Hobbes, whose pioneering work *Leviathan* had been published in 1651, less than twenty years earlier. In *Leviathan* Hobbes had put forward the pessimistic view that without government "the life of man [is] solitary, poor, nasty, brutish and short." Human beings had found this state of nature unbearable and had congregated in governed societies to overcome it. Any form of government was better than none, and thus we should obey whoever is in charge.

Spinoza took a more benevolent view of humanity, and his political theory was essentially liberal. Instead of supporting the state at all costs, he believed that the state, or its sovereign, justifies its power only by guaranteeing the security of its citizens and allowing individuals "to develop their minds...and use their reason without restraint." The state was there only to protect the individual, who must be allowed to pursue his own ends. (In Spinoza's rather optimistic view, this involved mastering the passions and using reason to gain a deeper understanding of oneself and the world. Where the seventeenth-century version of the beer-fueled football hooligan or couch potato fitted into this is unclear.) Spinoza also rather ingenuously maintained that the state should be self-limiting in its powers. It must act in accord with reason, and this means granting full freedom of thought and opinion. But here he realistically discriminates between thought and action. We must be allowed the freedom to think what we like, but our actions may be constrained by the state. And by actions he here includes public expressions of thought in any way likely to rouse the mob.

Spinoza's political theory very much reflects his own situation in Holland. Here there was tolerant government and freedom of thought—within limits. Spinoza's thoughts often went beyond these limits, but he stoutly maintained his right to have such thoughts, if not to publish them. And just as in threatened seventeenth-century Holland, the government's prime duty should be to ensure as best it could the security of its citizens.

Spinoza's political thinking was far ahead of its time. To us it may appear somewhat naive in places—in its own time such near-utopianism was regarded as dangerous rubbish or little short of ridiculous. Yet the attitude that Spinoza adopted toward the state is very much in line with present-day thinking in the liberal democracies of the Westernized world. A person has a right to hold racist, sexist, or even offensive politically correct views, but is restrained from putting these into action. Rousing the mob to violence against private smokers is against the law.

When the *Tractatus* was finally published in 1670 it hardly helped Spinoza's cause. Suffice to quote one typical reviewer, who declared that the book was "forged in Hell by a renegade Jew and the Devil, and issued with the knowledge of Mr. Jan de Witt." (Jan de Witt was the Dutch statesman and opponent of the Royalists, whose political skills had helped protect Holland from the aggressive attentions of both England and France—a pet scapegoat among reactionaries for all the ills of the age.)

These were troubled times for Holland, and even Spinoza was not immune to events around him, as we can see from his political theories in the *Tractatus*. These contained a blend of quietism and impracticality—which nevertheless ensured that the *Tractatus* was banned four years after its publication. In 1665 the Dutch had become involved in a war against England. In this the Dutch did better than anyone since William the Conqueror (including Napoleon and Hitler). At one point they sailed up the Thames and the Medway, burned the English fleet, destroyed the naval yards, and seized the port of Sheerness. Dutch guns were audible even in London, where they caused a panic and prompted the diarist Samuel Pepys to make his will. A peace had been patched up with the help of Louis XIV, but in 1672 the French laid claim to the Spanish Netherlands (now Belgium) and invaded Holland. In the ensuing alarm and political turmoil, de Witt was set upon by the mob in The Hague and torn limb from limb. When Spinoza heard of this incident he became incandescent with rage. He immediately went to his room and made a placard, on which he wrote "the very lowest of barbarians." This was his description of the mob which had murdered de Witt. Spinoza intended to march through the streets and publicly hang his placard on the wall at the very spot where de Witt's murder had taken place. This act of suicidal foolhardiness was fortunately prevented when his landlord discovered what he was up to, and locked him in his room.

By this time Spinoza was living within the city limits of The Hague. His first residence in the city center had been a room at 32 Stille Verkade, which in those days had been on the quayside of a canal that is now filled in. (Some twenty-five years later Spinoza's early biographer, the pastor Celerus, was to live in this very room while writing his invaluable work.) But this room had proved too expensive for Spinoza (though not his biographer, as is often the case with the biographers of genius), and Spinoza had moved to another room on Paviljoensgracht, in a house owned by the painter van der Spijk. This house is now maintained as a Spinoza museum, and it's possible to see the paneled room, with its old beamed ceiling and small mirror beside the window, where Spinoza lived during the last decade of his life.

According to Celerus, who gathered material for his biography from people who remembered Spinoza when he was alive, the philosopher was always meticulously dressed despite his poverty. Yet according to another source: "as for his Cloaths he was very careless of 'em, and they were no better than those of the meanest citizen." Tramp or dandy? Judging from his portraits, Spinoza probably dressed indifferently, at the frayed-cuffs level of gentility.

Spinoza went on grinding his lenses and writing. He began a Hebrew grammar, which he was never to finish. But he did succeed in completing a *Treatise on the Rainbow,* a subject which seems to have held a curious fascination for the great philosophers of the period. Descartes, Spinoza, and Leibniz all wrote on the rainbow—and though this was not a traditional philosophical subject, and there was thus no need for them to maintain the philosophic tradition of getting it wrong, all of them managed to do so.

By now Spinoza's works were being circulated privately, and a group met regularly in The Hague to discuss his ideas. Among this group was a wealthy medical student called de Vries. When de Vries learned that Spinoza was ill and likely soon to die, he decided to leave Spinoza a gift of 2,000 florins and an annuity of 500 florins. But Spinoza refused to accept this gift, and insisted that the annuity be reduced to 300 florins. He appears to have become rather paranoid about compromising his intellectual independence, and went on eking out a living grinding his lenses. By now he had become a respected thinker throughout Europe (his accolades from the religious authorities alone spoke for themselves), and several celebrated intellectual figures came to visit him in his dusty, spider-webbed room.

The most interesting of these was Ehrenfried Walter van Tschirnhaus, the German scientist, who together with his alchemist assistant discovered how to make hard porcelain, which went into production at Meissen in the early eighteenth-century, just too late to make him a fortune (he died in 1708). Another visitor was Leibniz, at the time the only other philosophic mind on a par with Spinoza in continental Europe. Spinoza discussed his ideas with Leibniz and even showed him a copy of the *Ethics* as well as other unpublished papers. Leibniz was so impressed by this unpublished material that as soon as he returned home to Germany he began plagiarizing it.

In 1673 Spinoza was offered the chair of philosophy at the University of Heidelberg by the local ruler, Count Palatine Carl Ludwig. The post was offered on condition that the philosophy Spinoza taught would not contravene the teachings of the church (which shows how much Count Carl had read of Spinoza's philosophy). Spinoza had the sense to turn down this prestigious post.

Spinoza continued to correspond with a wide range of eminent intellectuals. These included his old friend Heinrich Oldenburg, whom he had first met at Rijnsburg. Several years earlier Oldenburg had been appointed first secretary of the Royal Society in London. No one had seemed to object to this Dutch citizen continuing in his post throughout England's war against Holland. Nor did anyone appear to find it odd that he continued to correspond with his Dutch friend Spinoza in Holland. The war delayed the mail a bit but didn't otherwise interfere with regular communication between the two pen pals. Surprisingly their exchange of abstruse ideas, which would have appeared to any censor worth his salt as an obvious code, led to no suspicion that either was a spy. You had to do far more (or less) in those days to attract such attention, as Spinoza was soon to discover.

In May 1673 Spinoza received an invitation from the French statesman Condé to visit him in Utrecht and discuss his ideas. Utrecht was only thirty miles away, but at the time it was under French occupation. Spinoza was given papers granting him safe conduct and set off to meet this brilliant man, who was a friend of Molière and Racine. When Spinoza arrived in

Utrecht he discovered that Condé had been called away on state business. After hanging around for a few weeks (doubtless baffling the French chefs with his demands for milk sops and raisin gruel), Spinoza finally returned to The Hague—where rumors quickly began to spread that he was a French spy. Things soon took a dangerous turn. (It was only a year since the de Witt lynching.) Spinoza decided that the answer to these rumors was quite simple: he would go into the street and announce to the mob that he was certainly not a spy. Fortunately his long-suffering landlord once again managed to lock him up in the nick of time, and eventually the affair blew over.

To this day there remains an element of mystery surrounding this episode. It has been seriously suggested that Spinoza was sent to conduct secret political negotiations with Condé on behalf of the Dutch government. But under the fraught and delicate political circumstances of the time, this is unthinkable. What is just possible is that Spinoza was so unlikely an emissary that he was ordered to undertake the journey and entrusted with some kind of secret message.

Spinoza was now in his early forties. The long hard nights of lonely thought, and eking out a day-to-day living on the cash he earned from lens-grinding, were beginning to take their toll on his weak constitution. It seems likely that his lungs were affected by constantly inhaling ground glass. He began to suffer from phthisis, a wasting disease associated with tuberculosis. By the summer of 1676 Spinoza's frail, consumptive figure was seen less and less about the quarter, and when winter set in he took to his bed. His health began to fade rapidly.

Spinoza died on Sunday, February 21, 1677, while his landlord was at church. At the time Spinoza was being attended by his longtime friend Dr. Meyer. There's a curious story that after Spinoza died, Dr. Meyer disappeared with the loose change on Spinoza's table and a silver-handled knife. This seems preposterous, though it may just be possible. And just as possible that the kleptomaniac doctor also managed to filch Spinoza's entire stock of several hundred unfinished lenses, which later fell into the hands of the canny antique dealer Cornelius van Halewijn.

Either way, most people had the impression that there wasn't much left when Spinoza died. Even his greedy half-sister Rebekah decided that this time there was nothing worth going to court over. But these reports conflict with other evidence, which states that Spinoza left a library of 160 books, "the catalogue of which has been preserved." Such a collection would have fetched a tidy sum in those days, when leather-bound books were used even for reading as well as decor. Spinoza also left a number of unpublished works, including the masterpiece for which he will always be remembered, the *Ethics*. These works and his letters were published as his *Opera Posthuma* (Posthumous Works) in the very year that he died. But they were published anonymously, as Spinoza specifically decreed that he wished there to be no doctrine named after him. According to the executor of his will: "In the 11th definition of the Passions [in Spinoza's *Ethics*] where he explains the nature of ambition, he plainly charges with vainglory those who do after this sort."

In the following year the authorities did their best to deny Spinoza's last wishes by attracting as much attention to his *Opera Posthuma* as they could. Spinoza's work was identified with its author and banned, on the grounds that it "labefacted" the faith and "vilipended the authenticity of miracles." His entire work was declared "profane, atheistic, and blasphemous." Spinozism was born. And just to help it on its way, a few years later the French encyclopedist Bayle defined Spinozism in his *Dictionaire* as "the most monstrous hypothesis imaginable, the most absurd." (A sadly illiberal view, coming from another who had found it expedient to live in tolerant Holland on account of his beliefs.) This high-level criticism of Spinoza's work continued well into the next century, when no less than Hume described it as "a hideous hypothesis."

Oblivious to such criticism in death, as he probably was in life, Spinoza lies buried in

Neukirk in Dam Square in the center of Amsterdam.

Afterword

Spinoza made the mistake of viewing the world rationally, when of course it is nothing of the sort, either in fact or ultimately. (Modern mathematical scientists fall into a similar error when they view it mathematically.) Philosophers before Spinoza naively tended to view the world from the human viewpoint. Philosophers after him have persisted in this approach, with increasing awareness of its limitations. Spinoza, on the other hand, dispensed with the human viewpoint, choosing to see the world *sub specie aeternitatis* (beneath the gaze of eternity). Nowadays philosophers and scientists alike accept the futility of searching for any ultimate truth. Such "truths" as we can discover can only be "ours," that is to say, from our point of view. Any ultimate objective yardstick is inconceivable and unspeakable. "God is dead" also means that eternity is blind.

Spinoza pointed out that the pursuit of reason would "disenchant" the world. By this he meant that reason would strip it of its sacred as well as its superstitious aspects. He saw this as only a stage in our understanding of ourselves and the world. If we pursued rational thought to its next stage, we would rediscover God in a "religion of disenchantment." This proved too much for the religious authorities of Spinoza's day, who suspected that most rationalists would remain at the first stage. Their suspicions have more than been confirmed. Most scientists today remain in Spinoza's novice stage of rational development. And even those who arrive at a "religion of disenchantment" remain beyond the pale of all religious orthodoxy, with the possible exception of Buddhism. But then so did Spinoza. Indeed, it is difficult to see precisely what Spinoza meant by this "religion of disenchantment."

A universal God who can be properly apprehended only by the application of reason to the world around us? This suggests that Spinoza's "religion of disenchantment" could in fact be a prescient description of modern science: a pantheistic universe whose truth we can apprehend only by the use of reason, mathematics, and rational experiment: a god-world where number is prayer. This may be what Spinoza had in mind, and indeed it may be a beautiful poetic description of modern science seen *sub specie aeternitatis*. Unfortunately is it not how most modern scientists regard the universe.

The rationalism introduced by Descartes was brought to its epitome by Spinoza. Yet within a dozen years of Spinoza's death, rationalism was superseded by empiricism, as put forward by the British philosopher John Locke. The belief that ultimately the truth can be discovered by reason gave way to the belief that the only way we can know the truth is by experience.

The counterwave of German metaphysics in the nineteenth century saw a revival of Spinoza's stock on the philosophical exchange. This was largely unfortunate. The clear rationalism of Spinoza's system was to inspire Hegel to an even more vast system, where steepled clarity was replaced with gargoyled German metaphysics. Spinoza equally inspired the Marxism that grew out of Hegelianism (as an inversion of it). Yet dialectical materialism remains but a *lumpen* shadow of Spinoza's geometric pantheism.

Spinoza's influence continues. Some modern mathematicians who otherwise view philosophy with contempt retain a soft spot for him. Alas, his belief in a certain rational universe contains built-in self-contradictions similar to their own belief in a certain mathematical universe. The systematic explanation of the world has crumpled into a rubble of relativisms. We live in the post-wall era of Humpty Dumpty, where Spinoza's philosophy is but a poetic dream. Yet it remains one of the finest ever produced.

From Spinoza's Writings

The first eight definitions, upon which Spinoza based the "geometric" proof of his system:

I. By CAUSE OF ITSELF (*causa sui*) I understand that whose essence involves existence; or that whose nature cannot be conceived except as existing.

II. A thing is said to be FINITE IN ITS KIND (*in suo genere finita*) when it can be limited by another thing of the same nature. For example, a body is said to be finite because we can always conceive of another body larger than it. Similarly, thought is limited by another thought. But body cannot be limited by thought, nor thought by body.

III. By SUBSTANCE (*substantia*) I understand that which is in itself and is conceived through itself. That is, that the conception of which does not depend upon the conception of another thing, from which it has to be formed.

IV. By ATTRIBUTE (*attributum*) I understand that which the intellect perceives of substance as constituting its essence.

V. By MODE (*modus*) I understand the modification of substance; that which is in something else, through which it is also conceived.

VI. By GOD (*Deus*) I understand an absolutely infinite being; that is, substance consisting of infinite attributes, each of which expresses eternal and infinite essence.

VII. A thing is said to be FREE (*libera*) which exists solely through the necessity of its own nature, and is determined into action by itself alone. That thing is said to be NECESSARY (*necessaria*), or rather COMPELLED (*coacta*), which is determined by something else to exist and act in a certain definite and determinate way.

VIII. I understand ETERNITY (*aeternitas*) in so

far as it is conceived as following necessarily from the definition of an eternal thing.

—*Ethics,* Part 1, Opening Definitions

An example of Spinoza's thoroughgoing pantheism:
Apart from God, no substance can exist or be conceived.

—*Ethics,* Part 1, Proposition 14

Another proof of God's existence:
Because the ability to exist is a power, it follows that the more reality belongs to the nature of a thing, the more power it has of itself to exist. Therefore an absolutely infinite being, or God, has of himself an absolutely infinite power of existing. Thus he exists absolutely.

—*Ethics,* Part 1

Examples of Spinoza's all-embracing determinism:
God is the cause of all things, which are in him.
—*Ethics,* Part 1

There is nothing contingent in nature, but all things are from the necessity of the divine nature determined to exist and to act in a definite way.
—*Ethics,* Part 1

When people think they are free, they are deceived. They hold to this opinion only because they are conscious of their actions but remain ignorant of what actually causes these actions.
—*Ethics,* Part 2

The two attributes:
Mind and body are one and the same individual which is conceived now under the attribute of thought, and now under the attribute of extension.
—*Ethics,* Part 2

Spinoza's idea of government—far in advance of its time, if a trifle utopian:

The ultimate aim of government is not to rule or restrain by fear, not to exact obedience, but on the contrary, to free every man from fear, so that he is able to live in the greatest possible security; in other words, to strengthen his natural right to exist and go about his business without injury to himself or to others. The object of government is not to change men from rational beings into beasts or puppets, but to enable them to develop their minds and bodies in security, and to use their reason without restraint; without showing hatred, anger, or deceit, nor watched with the eyes of jealousy and injustice. In effect, the true aim of government is liberty.

—*Tractatus Theologico-Politicus,* Chapter 20

Chronology of Significant Philosophical Dates

6th C B.C.	The beginning of Western philosophy with Thales of Miletus.
End of 6th C B.C.	Death of Pythagoras.
399 B.C.	Socrates sentenced to death in Athens.
c 387 B.C.	Plato founds the Academy in Athens, the first university.
335 B.C.	Aristotle founds the Lyceum in Athens, a rival school to the Academy.

324 A.D.	Emperor Constantine moves capital of Roman Empire to Byzantium.
400 A.D.	St. Augustine writes his *Confessions*. Philosophy absorbed into Christian theology.
410 A.D.	Sack of Rome by Visigoths heralds opening of Dark Ages.
529 A.D.	Closure of Academy in Athens by Emperor Justinian marks end of Hellenic thought.
Mid-13th C	Thomas Aquinas writes his commentaries on Aristotle. Era of Scholasticism.
1453	Fall of Byzantium to Turks, end of Byzantine Empire.
1492	Columbus reaches America. Renaissance in Florence and revival of interest in Greek learning.
1543	Copernicus publishes *On the Revolution of the Celestial Orbs*, proving mathematically that the earth revolves around the sun.

1633	Galileo forced by church to recant heliocentric theory of the universe.
1641	Descartes publishes his *Meditations*, the start of modern philosophy.
1677	Death of Spinoza allows publication of his *Ethics*.
1687	Newton publishes *Principia*, introducing concept of gravity.
1689	Locke publishes *Essay Concerning Human Understanding*. Start of empiricism.
1710	Berkeley publishes *Principles of Human Knowledge*, advancing empiricism to new extremes.
1716	Death of Leibniz.
1739–1740	Hume publishes *Treatise of Human Nature*, taking empiricism to its logical limits.
1781	Kant, awakened from his "dogmatic slumbers" by Hume, publishes *Critique of Pure Reason*.

Great era of German metaphysics begins.

1807   Hegel publishes *The Phenomenology of Mind*, high point of German metaphysics.

1818   Schopenhauer publishes *The World as Will and Representation*, introducing Indian philosophy into German metaphysics.

1889   Nietzsche, having declared "God is dead," succumbs to madness in Turin.

1921   Wittgenstein publishes *Tractatus Logico-Philosophicus*, claiming the "final solution" to the problems of philosophy.

1920s   Vienna Circle propounds Logical Positivism.

1927   Heidegger publishes *Being and Time*, heralding split between analytical and Continental philosophy.

1943   Sartre publishes *Being and Nothingness*, advancing

Heidegger's thought and instigating existentialism.

1953   Posthumous publication of Wittgenstein's *Philosophical Investigations*. High era of linguistic analysis.

Chronology of Spinoza's Life

1632	Spinoza born in Amsterdam.
1646	Birth of Leibniz.
1648	End of Thirty Years War, leaving large areas of Germany and central Europe devastated.
1650	Death of Descartes.
1654	Death of Spinoza's father and ensuing lawsuit against his sister.
1655	Unsuccessful attempt to assassinate Spinoza.
1656	Excommunicated by Jewish authorities.

1660	Goes to live at village of Rijnsburg, outside Leiden.
1663	Moves to the Hague.
1663–1665	Writing *Ethics*.
1670	*Tractatus Theologico-Politicus* published anonymously.
1673	Turns down offer of chair of philosophy at University of Heidelberg.
1675	Completes *Ethics*.
1676	Visited by German philosopher Leibniz.
1677	Spinoza dies at The Hague. Publication of his masterwork, *Ethics*.

Recommended Reading

Frederick Copleston, *History of Philosophy,* Vol. 4: *Descartes to Leibniz* (Doubleday, 1994). Contains five chapters on Spinoza's life and ideas.

Don Garrett, ed., *The Cambridge Companion to Spinoza* (Cambridge University Press, 1995). A wide range of essays on Spinoza and related topics by various Spinoza experts.

Roger Scruton, *Spinoza* (Oxford University Press, 1986). A short work in the Past Masters series, the best brief critique of Spinoza's ideas.

The Ethics of Spinoza (Carol Publishing Group, 1995). His seminal work on his metaphysical system and his ethics, couched in the Euclidian style.

Baruch Spinoza, *Tractatus Theologico-Politicus,* 2nd

ed. (E. J. Brill, 1991). Contains his political system amidst biblical commentary.

Index

A NOTE ON THE AUTHOR

Paul Strathern has lectured in philosophy and mathematics and now lives and writes in London. A Somerset Maugham prize winner, he is also the author of books on history and travel as well as five novels. His articles have appeared in a great many publications, including the *Observer* (London) and the *Irish Times*. His own degree in philosophy was earned at Trinity College, Dublin.